# CELEBRITY ACTIVISTS™

# MICHAEL J. FOX

## PARKINSON'S DISEASE RESEARCH ADVOCATE

**ROSEN**
PUBLISHING®
New York

**SIMONE PAYMENT**

Published in 2009 by The Rosen Publishing Group, Inc.
29 East 21st Street, New York, NY 10010

Copyright © 2009 by The Rosen Publishing Group, Inc.

First Edition

**Library of Congress Cataloging-in-Publication Data**

Payment, Simone.
Michael J. Fox: Parkinson's disease research advocate / Simone Payment.—1st ed.
      p. cm.—(Celebrity activists)
Includes bibliographical references.
ISBN-13: 978-1-4042-1765-2 (library binding)
1. Fox, Michael J., 1961– —Health. 2. Parkinson's disease—Patients—United States—Biography. 3. Health reformers—United States—Biography. 4. Television actors and actresses—United States—Biography. I. Title.
RC382.F69 2009
362.196'8330092—dc22
[B]

2007048654

*Manufactured in Malaysia*

**On the cover:** Inset: Michael J. Fox. Background: Research being done on stem cells.

# CONTENTS

# INTRODUCTION

Most people would say that Michael J. Fox was leading a charmed life. He grew up in a happy family and was popular, did well in school, played guitar in a band, and excelled at hockey. He began working as a professional actor when he was just a teenager in his hometown of Vancouver, British Columbia, Canada. When he was eighteen years old, he moved to Los Angeles, California, to seek fame and fortune in Hollywood, and when he was in his early twenties, he landed the role that would make him a household name: Alex P. Keaton on the popular television situation comedy *Family Ties*.

Michael J. Fox has successfully transformed himself from a world-famous actor to a well-respected activist. His foundation has raised millions of dollars to fund Parkinson's disease research.

Parts in movies followed, including Fox's starring role in the three *Back to the Future* movies. Fox was living the high life in a nice house in Los Angeles, driving his fleet of fast cars, and partying with his celebrity friends. He settled down when he met the love of his life, Tracy Pollan, and they married and had a son.

When Fox was just thirty years old, however, he got some startling news: he had Parkinson's disease. Parkinson's is a movement disorder that occurs when the brain does not produce enough dopamine, a chemical that helps the brain give "directions" to the rest of the body. People with Parkinson's shake or twitch involuntarily and can have problems with muscle stiffness and with walking and talking. Fox's diagnosis was particularly startling because Parkinson's normally strikes people twice Fox's age at the time.

Although Fox was shocked by his diagnosis, he brushed it off at first. His natural optimism helped him avoid worrying too much about what problems the disease would cause him down the road. In the first few years after he was diagnosed with Parkinson's, Fox was able to control many of the symptoms of his disease with medication, and he kept the diagnosis secret, telling only his family and a few close friends. Fox continued to act in movies and then in *Spin City*, another popular television situation comedy. Fox and Pollan also added to their family, having twin daughters.

Seven years after his diagnosis, Fox realized he could no longer keep his Parkinson's disease a secret. Controlling his symptoms with medication was no longer as effective, and the strain of keeping his diagnosis from people became too much. Fox revealed his diagnosis in 1999. He was shocked by the outpouring of support and good wishes he received from people around the world. Fox was also surprised at the amount of attention Parkinson's disease received as a result. The general public became much more aware of the disease and its effects. Hundreds of people with Parkinson's got in touch with Fox to thank him for bringing attention to the disease.

Fox decided his status as a well-known actor gave him the perfect opportunity to make a difference to millions of people around the world who have Parkinson's. So, in 2000, he embarked on a new phase of his life and became a Parkinson's activist.

He started the Michael J. Fox Foundation for Parkinson's Research, which has so far raised more than $90 million to fund research for a cure for the disease. Fox's goal is to cure Parkinson's by the year 2010, and he won't stop working hard until his goal is achieved.

# CHAPTER ONE

## "He's Going to Do Things You Can't Even Imagine"

When Michael J. Fox was young, his grandmother predicted he'd be famous someday. Because his grandmother was known for her ability to predict future events, everyone in Fox's family had little doubt that she would be proved correct.

Michael Andrew Fox was born June 9, 1961, in Edmonton, Alberta, Canada. The Fox family already consisted of two girls, Karen and Jacqueline, and one boy, Steven. Another girl, Kelli, would complete the family three years after Michael was born.

Michael's father, Bill Fox Jr., was an encryption and decoding specialist in the Royal Canadian Army Signal Corps. Because Bill Fox was in the military, the Fox family moved often when Michael was young. They finally settled in Burnaby, British Columbia (just outside Vancouver), when Michael was ten years old. Many relatives lived in and around Burnaby, and the Fox family was close and happy.

Phyllis, Michael's mother, took care of the five Fox children. Keeping track of five children was not an easy task, particularly where Michael was concerned. Even at a very young age, he was liable to wander off on adventures. One day, when he was just two years old, Michael left the house by himself and was later found by a neighbor. Later that same day, he made his way to a candy store that he must have noticed on his first trip around the neighborhood. On his second trip, he took a pile of money his father had left on a counter so he could buy candy.

Bright, inquisitive, and friendly, Michael charmed his family and later his teachers and schoolmates. He had little trouble making friends when he started a new school each time the Fox family moved.

Even before he went to school, he was a voracious reader and loved to draw and paint. He wrote poems and stories when he was only five years old. Michael also loved to ride his bike and hunt for creatures like snakes and frogs in local ponds and meadows.

Although Michael was very smart sometimes, he had a hard time paying attention in school. In his early years of school, he got good grades despite his occasional inability to focus on schoolwork. Michael was also very small for his age. In fact, he was sometimes mistaken for Kelli's twin brother even though she was three years younger than he was. With his propensity to be distracted and his small stature, some of Michael's extended family worried about what would happen to him when he grew up.

Michael's grandmother, whom he called Nana, had no such worries. She was positive Michael would be famous someday and would repeatedly reassure the family that everything would work out for him. In *Lucky Man*, Fox's autobiography, he writes that his grandmother would tell the rest of the family, "He's going to do things you can't even imagine. And he'll probably be very famous one day." Michael was very close to Nana, and her death in 1972 was very hard on him.

## Finding His Niche

Because of Nana's prediction that he would be famous someday, Michael believed it, too. However, at the time that Nana made her prediction, he had no idea that he'd find fame as an actor. Instead, he thought maybe he'd be a star hockey player—despite all the broken teeth and stitches he accumulated while playing the sport.

In junior high school, Michael continued to be good at writing and drawing. He also loved music. One year he got a guitar for Christmas. He taught himself to play by listening to his brother's records. He also took a music class at school. There, he met Andy Hill, a student one year older than he was. They discovered they loved the same music— including Aerosmith, Bachman-Turner Overdrive, and Led Zeppelin. They decided to form a band, which they called Halex (after a brand of Ping-Pong balls). Halex played at high school dances and even at some bars, despite the fact that the two

Michael J. Fox dreamed of playing hockey professionally in the National Hockey League (NHL), but by high school he had focused on acting instead.

band members were much too young to legally buy a drink.

Besides his musical talent, Michael discovered another talent in junior high school: acting. Almost from the first day of drama class, Michael found it very easy not only to memorize lines but also to become the character he was playing. His drama teacher thought he was very talented and could take his acting beyond school plays.

In high school, Michael continued to act in school plays and perform with Halex some nights and weekends. He got good grades in artistic classes like English and drama, but he did not do well in math and science, much to his father's dismay. However, his father was proud of his band and his obvious acting talent.

Early in 1977, when Michael was a sophomore in high school, his drama teacher, Ross Jones, told him about a casting call for a television show called *Leo and Me*. The Canadian Broadcasting Corporation (CBC) in nearby Vancouver was going to make the show, and it was looking for a twelve-year-old to play one of the starring roles. Even though Michael was already sixteen years old at the time, being very small for his age worked to his advantage, and he was chosen to play the part.

Michael's first professional acting role turned into two professional acting roles when the producers of *Leo and Me* offered him the lead part in a television movie being shot that summer. Michael accepted both roles and loved working on the television show and the movie. He particularly enjoyed meeting all the people who worked with him in front of, and behind, the camera. He also loved that he made $6,000 on both roles—a large sum of money for a teenager in 1977.

## High School, Cut Short

When Michael returned to high school in the fall of 1977 for his junior year, he was busy with acting work he had gotten on other shows on CBC and in commercials. He didn't devote much time to school-work his junior year, and this continued into the fall of his senior year. By that time, he was flunking most of his classes—even drama. This was mostly because he rarely made it to class. In the fall of his senior year, he was acting at night in a play in Vancouver and was often too tired the next morning to make it to class.

Because he was doing poorly in most—if not all—of his classes, Michael's parents knew something had to be done if he was to graduate from high school. That fall, they met with school officials to ask if Michael could get credit for all of the out-of-school experience he was getting through his acting jobs. They also suggested that he could get tutoring to make up the work that he had missed. School officials refused these suggestions, so Michael's parents decided to allow Michael to drop out of school at the end of the fall of 1978.

## Off to Hollywood

After dropping out of high school, Michael continued to act in plays and commercials in and around Vancouver, but by the spring of 1979, he was ready for a bigger challenge. That challenge was Hollywood, and luckily, his parents agreed that he should take a shot at making a career out of his acting talent. In April, Michael's dad drove him to Hollywood, California, to meet with agents who could help him get work in television and movies. Every single agent they met with wanted to represent him. Michael chose the agent who promised to get him a

## Becoming Michael J. Fox

To act in Hollywood, you must join the Screen Actors Guild (SAG), and when Fox applied, he found that there was already a "Michael Fox" in SAG. He would need to change his name. At first, he considered using his middle initial and going by "Michael A. Fox," but he decided that he didn't want people thinking of him as "Michael, a fox." He remembered an actor he admired named Michael J. Pollard and decided to use "J" as his middle initial.

role in a Disney movie. The movie was called *Midnight Madness*, and it began shooting on June 10, 1979, the day after Michael's eighteenth birthday.

Fox was on his own in Hollywood, and at first things went well for him. After he finished *Midnight Madness*, he got parts guest starring in television shows like *Family* and *Trapper John, M.D.* He also got small parts in other movies and a role in a television series called *Palmerstown, U.S.A.*

Happy to be making a career out of his acting talent, Fox enjoyed himself in Hollywood, even though he was living in a very small—and very dirty—apartment. He was having so much fun with his acting career that he stopped paying attention to details like money, and he soon found that the managers he had hired to help him with his career had taken advantage of him and had kept more of his money than they should have.

Also, after the first few years in Hollywood, Fox was getting fewer and fewer acting jobs. By the spring of 1982, things were looking very bleak. He had begun selling his furniture just so he would have enough money to buy food and pay rent. His

One of Michael J. Fox's earliest movie roles was as a high school student in *Class of 1984*, a 1982 Canadian film.

A new-to-Hollywood Michael J. Fox made guest appearances on television programs. Here, he is pictured with Pernell Roberts on *Trapper John, M.D.* in 1981.

friends and family began encouraging him to return to Vancouver, at least for a while, but Fox didn't think his prospects in Vancouver looked particularly bright. What else did he know how to do besides act? Also, while working in Hollywood, Fox had not been paying taxes to the Internal Revenue Service and he worried that if he returned to Canada, he would have a hard time getting back into the United States due to his tax situation.

# CHAPTER TWO

## A Star Is Born

With no money in the bank and no steady acting work to pay the bills, Michael J. Fox was worried about whether he could continue pursuing his acting career in Hollywood. Just when his situation seemed to be at its worst, he auditioned for a new sitcom called *Family Ties*. The sitcom was about two former hippie parents and their three kids. Fox was trying out for the part of Alex P. Keaton, the oldest child, who, as a teenager, aspired to be rich and was a Republican—the exact opposite of his liberal parents.

Fox's first audition for *Family Ties* in March 1982 went well, but Gary David

Goldberg, the creator and producer of the show, didn't think Fox was right for the part. However, Judith Weiner, who was in charge of casting the show, was sure that Fox would be perfect and worked hard to convince Goldberg that Fox was the right person to play Alex. Weiner's pestering paid off, and Goldberg agreed to let Fox audition a second time. This time, he realized that Weiner was right. Fox was perfect, and Goldberg helped convince NBC, the television network that would be broadcasting the show, to hire him.

Michael Gross and Meredith Baxter-Birney played the *Family Ties* parents, and Justine Bateman and Tina Yothers played Fox's siblings. (Later in the show, a second son, played by Brian Bonsall, was added to the family.)

## A Hollywood Star

When *Family Ties* premiered in September 1982, it was not an immediate hit, but it did get Fox noticed. He was praised for his work on *Family Ties*, and movie parts began to come his way again. In 1983, he appeared in the television movie *High School U.S.A.*, where he met Nancy McKeon, star of the

The two-part episode "Alex Doesn't Live Here Anymore" ended the successful sitcom *Family Ties* in 1989. Fox is pictured here with *(from left)* Tina Yothers, Michael Gross, and Justine Bateman.

television show *The Facts of Life*. She and Fox began dating.

By 1984, *Family Ties* had become a television hit, and the popularity of the show had a lot to do with Fox's performance as the teenaged Alex. As the show's and Fox's popularity increased, movie producers began offering him more and bigger parts in movies. In the fall of 1984, while *Family Ties* was on a break due to Meredith Baxter-Birney's pregnancy, Fox filmed the 1985 movie *Teen Wolf*, in which he had the starring role.

A few months later, while Fox was back at work on *Family Ties*, Steven Spielberg offered him a part that would change his life: the role of Marty McFly in the first *Back to the Future* movie. Fox knew it was an opportunity too good to pass up, but because he was filming *Family Ties*, he had to shoot *Back to the Future* at night. During the winter of

Doc Brown (played by Christopher Lloyd) and Fox's character Marty McFly use a time-traveling car to send McFly back and forth in time in the 1985 blockbuster *Back to the Future*.

1985, Fox worked on the set of *Family Ties* from about 9:00 AM until 6:00 PM, and then a driver would take him to the *Back to the Future* set. When he could, Fox would take a nap during the drive. He would work on *Back to the Future* through the night, sometimes until 5:00 or 6:00 the next morning. Then he'd get a few hours of sleep before he'd have to head back to the *Family Ties* set by 9:00 AM. This was an exhausting schedule, but the months of working around the clock paid off when *Back to the Future* was released in July 1985 and was an instant success, making more than $300 million around the world.

As Fox's popularity increased even further due to his movie roles, the attention focused on *Family Ties* increased, too, and the television show got better and better ratings. Fox was recognized not just for his popularity as a movie star and teen idol; he was also getting accolades for his acting work. He received the 1986 Emmy for Best Lead Actor in a Comedy Series, along with still more roles in movies, such as *Light of Day* (1987), *The Secret of My Success* (1987), and *Bright Lights, Big City* (1989). Fox again won the Emmy for Best Lead Actor in a Comedy Series for

*Family Ties* in 1987 and 1988, and he won a Golden Globe award for his work on the series in 1989.

## Behind the Scenes

When he wasn't filming *Family Ties* or movies, Fox was living it up in Hollywood. He partied with friends and bought several fast cars and a large house. He was also enjoying the perks of fame, such as getting plenty of nice things—clothes, shoes, jewelry—for free. However, remembering his financial troubles earlier in his career, he was much more careful with his money this time around. He didn't want to end up broke again.

There were also lots of demands on his time. Fox had to do many publicity events, such as interviews on television talk shows, to promote his movies or *Family Ties*. However, whenever possible, he tried to balance those types of events with charity work, such as visits to children's hospitals.

During the 1985 season of *Family Ties,* the actress Tracy Pollan guest starred as Fox's girlfriend on the show. Pollan and Fox became good friends while working on seven episodes of *Family Ties* together. At the time, Fox was dating Nancy

Although Tracy Pollan played Fox's girlfriend in thirteen episodes of
*Family Ties*, they did not become a real-life couple until several years later.

McKeon, and Pollan was living with actor Kevin Bacon. Fox and Pollan were simply good friends, and after her episodes on *Family Ties* were completed, Pollan returned to New York City. However, the two met again in the spring of 1987 when Pollan auditioned for *Bright Lights, Big City*, which Fox was helping to cast as well as starring in. They were now both single, and when they began working on the movie, they soon began dating. Just a few months later, in December 1987, they got engaged.

Fox and Pollan were married on July 16, 1988, in what they had hoped would be a private ceremony in Vermont. The event was beautiful, but far from private—helicopters hired by tabloid magazines hovered overhead trying to get a picture of the two stars getting married. The following spring, on May 30, 1989, Pollan and Fox's son, Sam, was born.

Fox worked on the last season of *Family Ties* in 1989. Done with the television series, he had more time to shoot movies, and in the next few years, he made several, such as *Casualties of War* (1989), *Back to the Future II* (1989), and *Back to the Future III* (1990).

Fox remembers the filming of *Doc Hollywood* for the fun he and his castmates (including Woody Harrelson, pictured here with Fox) had after hours, but also because it marked the beginning of his Parkinson's diagnosis.

## Warning from a Pinkie

On November 13, 1990, Fox woke up in a motel room in Gainesville, Florida. He was there making the movie *Doc Hollywood*. He was startled to find that his left pinkie finger was twitching uncontrollably. Fox was slightly worried about this because he just could not make the finger stop moving. At first, he figured he'd slept on it. He took an aspirin—mostly to get rid of the headache he had from partying too much the night before. However, the pinkie continued to twitch, and as the day went on, he grew more worried, so he went to the University of Florida hospital that afternoon. A team of doctors examined him but could find nothing wrong. One of the doctors suggested that maybe he had hit his ulna, also known as the "funny bone."

Over the next days and weeks, his pinkie continued to twitch, and eventually the third and fourth fingers on his left hand began twitching as well. Fox noticed that he was having other problems on the left side of his body, including a stiff shoulder and an achy chest. But, he put off seeing a doctor. He was busy directing an episode of *Tales from the Crypt*, an HBO television series, and didn't want to take any time away.

Several months later, in August 1991, Fox was on vacation on Martha's Vineyard, an island off the coast of Massachusetts, with Pollan and Sam. While out jogging one day, he felt particularly stiff and tired, and the run took him longer than usual. Pollan grew concerned and drove the route Fox often ran to look for him. When she saw him, she noticed that the entire left side of his body was not moving normally. She and Fox decided it was time to see a doctor again.

Back in New York City, Fox visited a doctor who specialized in sports medicine. The doctor did tests and recommended physical therapy but also suggested that Fox go to see a neurologist. Fox made an appointment with one, and after running some tests, the doctor gave Fox some stunning news: he had Parkinson's disease.

At first, Fox had a very hard time comprehending the diagnosis. Parkinson's is a disease that most often appears in people fifty or older. Fox was only thirty years old at the time. Only about one in ten Parkinson's patients are diagnosed before the age of forty. In people this young, it is called young onset Parkinson's.

When Fox told Pollan about his diagnosis, they both cried. Fox spent a few days feeling sorry for himself. His family, too, was upset by the news. Fox went to several other doctors to get second opinions, but after doing extensive tests, all agreed that he had Parkinson's. Eventually, Fox's natural optimism took over, and he and Pollan decided that they would just have to deal with whatever happened as a result of the disease.

Even though Fox took an optimistic approach to his diagnosis, he immediately made the decision to tell only family and very close friends. He didn't want the public—or movie studio executives—to know. He didn't want people to feel sorry for him. And, more important, he was worried that movie studios would decide not to hire him to make movies if they knew. When he was diagnosed, the doctor told him he could probably act for another ten years. This worried Fox because that didn't seem like very much time—even though he had always planned to retire from acting when he turned forty.

## What Is Parkinson's Disease?

Parkinson's is a disease that affects movement. It can cause tremors (shaking), stiffness, difficulty with balance, and several other problems. It occurs when cells in the basal ganglia, the part of the brain that controls movement, become damaged. When they are healthy, these cells, called nigral cells, produce a chemical called dopamine. Dopamine is a chemical substance called a neurotransmitter, and it helps brain cells relay messages from the brain to the rest of the body. However, in people who have Parkinson's, the nigral cells become damaged and die, cutting down the production of dopamine. This disrupts the brain's ability to send the signals that control movement.

The damage to the nigral cells does not happen all at once. In fact, in the earliest stages of Parkinson's

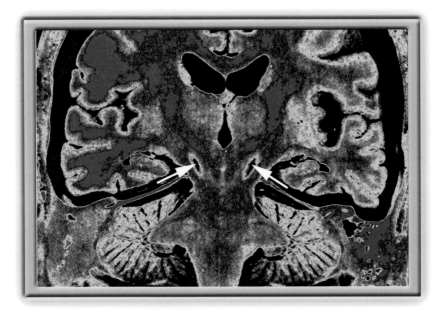

Parkinson's disease affects the part of the brain called the substantia nigra (indicated by the arrows), which produces the neurotransmitter dopamine.

disease, although nigral cells are dying, other cells continue to produce dopamine. It's not until the level of dopamine in the brain is down by 60 to 80 percent that symptoms appear. When symptoms do begin to appear, they come on slowly and gradually get worse. This is why Parkinson's is called a progressive disease. Fox probably had the disease for five or more years before his diagnosis, but the disease progressed very slowly in his case; this is probably because he was very young when first diagnosed. The disease tends to speed up as patients get older.

A shaking hand is usually the symptom that leads someone to see a doctor, just as in Fox's case. There is no specific test that doctors can perform that will tell them for sure if someone has Parkinson's. So, at first doctors do tests to rule out other diseases or conditions that might cause a person's symptoms. If they find that symptoms aren't caused by something else, doctors ask patients a list of questions about their ability to function, their memory, and their emotions, and perform an exam to look for other physical signs. This set of questions and the medical exam is called the Unified Parkinson's Disease Rating Scale, or UPDRS. It is a good test when given by skilled doctors, but it is not conclusive. If a doctor, after performing some of the usual diagnostic tests, thinks a patient has Parkinson's, he or she will give the patient a drug called levodopa, and if this drug makes symptoms improve, the patient almost surely has Parkinson's disease.

Not every Parkinson's patient has exactly the same symptoms, and not everyone's symptoms develop in the same way. In fact, Parkinson's disease

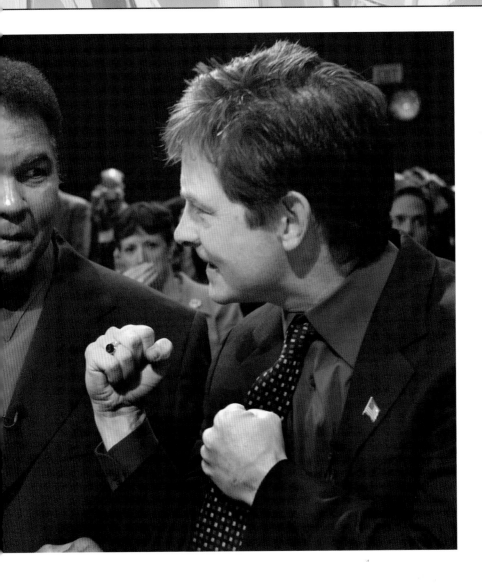

Parkinson's patients Muhammad Ali and Michael J. Fox testified at a Senate hearing in Washington, D.C., on May 22, 2002. The two have also made public service announcements together to call attention to the need for more funding for Parkinson's research.

## Dealing with His Diagnosis

In the first few months after Fox was diagnosed with Parkinson's, he tried not to let the news get him down. He hired a personal trainer to help keep him in shape and as healthy as possible. But, at the same time, he was also drinking a lot to help him forget about his diagnosis. In the spring of 1992, he realized his drinking was out of control and that he would need to stop. He quit drinking, which helped his situation, but he felt depressed through much of the rest of that year and well into the next. He made a few movies, but he wasn't getting very good roles and wasn't enjoying himself as an actor or with his family. Late in 1993, he again decided things would have to change, so he started going to a counselor who helped him realize that he couldn't ignore his Parkinson's. He would need to face up to his diagnosis.

Facing the fact that he had Parkinson's also meant getting better medical care. Fox was taking a medication called Sinemet (a form of levodopa) to help stop the left side of his body from shaking. This allowed him to work for several hours at a time without anyone being able to see his symptoms.

Sinemet is a drug used to treat Parkinson's symptoms by helping the brain produce more dopamine, the substance the brain needs to send messages to the rest of the body.

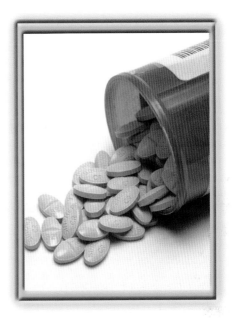

This was how he kept anyone from finding out that he had Parkinson's. However, while the medication could keep his symptoms under control for a time, it would wear off after a while. Also, it was difficult to regulate the dosage of the medication and to figure out how long it would take for a pill to start working. Fox had stopped going to neurologists and was getting his Sinemet from his regular doctor, making up the medication dosage and timing as he went along.

In 1994, Fox decided that it would be better to see a neurologist who could help him regulate his medication. He went to Dr. Allan Ropper, who got Fox back on track with his drug treatments. Life began to improve for Fox throughout 1994, and that year he also took—and passed—the General Equivalency Diploma (GED) exam. Sixteen years after dropping out of high school, he was finally a high school graduate.

## Spin City

With the help of his medication, Fox was still keeping his diagnosis under wraps. In the winter of 1995, he decided he wanted to return to working in television. His twin daughters, Aquinnah and Schuyler, had been born February 15, and Fox hoped to find work that he could do from New York City where he and his family lived most of the time.

Fox met with Gary David Goldberg, creator and producer of *Family Ties*, about a new project. Goldberg was planning to work on a sitcom about the deputy mayor of New York City. Fox and Goldberg agreed it was the perfect role for the actor, and they started filming the show, called *Spin City*, in New York City in the fall of 1996.

*Spin City* was another hit for Fox and Goldberg, and Fox enjoyed being back at work on a television series. He also enjoyed being able to spend a lot of time with his family when not on the set of the show.

He was able to control his Parkinson's symptoms by taking his medication at key times, such as before rehearsals or tapings of the show. However, still wanting to keep the diagnosis a secret, he sometimes had to wait in his dressing room until the medication began to work.

Eventually, however, Fox found that Sinemet was not working as well as it once had. It was becoming more and more difficult for him to hide the symptoms at work. The symptoms were also interfering with life with his family, making it difficult for him to even read a book to his son and young twins because his hand shook so much. Dr. Ropper suggested that he have surgery to help stop his symptoms. The surgery Fox and Dr. Ropper chose is called a thalamotomy, However, by having the surgery, Fox risked becoming paralyzed or losing the ability to speak.

Fox decided the surgery was worth the risk, and Dr. Bruce Cook performed the thalamotomy on March 15, 1998, at a hospital outside Boston, Massachusetts. Dr. Cook operated on Fox on a Sunday morning so there was less chance that people would see Fox before or after his surgery.

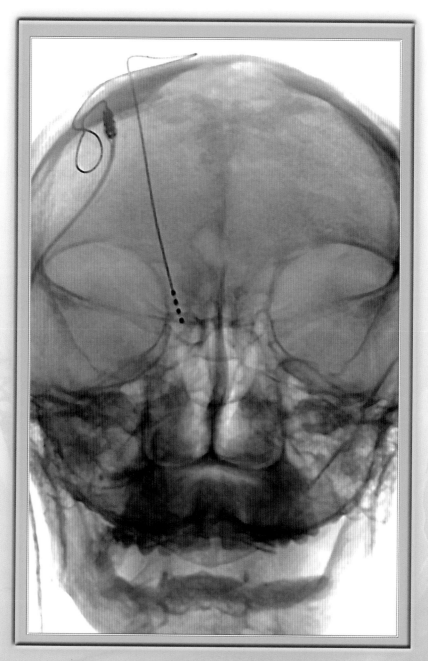

This X-ray shows an electrode implanted in the brain of a Parkinson's patient to electrically stimulate the thalamus, helping to control tremors.

The surgery turned out to be a great success: Fox's left side stopped shaking. However, soon after the surgery, Fox noticed that his right hand had begun to shake just a little. Fox had to take that new development in stride. He wrote in his autobiography, *Lucky Man*, "After all I'd been through, after all I'd learned and all that I'd been given, I was going to do what I had been doing every day for the last few years: just show up and do the best that I could with whatever lay in front of me."

# CHAPTER THREE

## A Different Kind of Spotlight

From the time he learned he had Parkinson's in 1991, Michael J. Fox had spent lots of time and energy keeping his diagnosis a secret from the public, and even from people he knew and saw every day.

It took a lot of effort to regulate his medication so that he'd never be seen showing any symptoms of Parkinson's disease in public. This caused him problems at work, when he would sometimes have to reschedule meetings or delay filming of his movies or *Spin City*. But for seven years, he kept his secret from his fellow actors, his colleagues in television, and even many of those in his private life.

## A Difficult Decision

In 1998, Fox began to think about revealing the secret he had kept for so long. In January of that year, he attended the Golden Globes awards ceremony in Hollywood, where he won the Golden Globe for Best Performance by an Actor in a TV Series—Comedy/Musical. However, when he arrived at the ceremony, he had to ask the driver of his limousine to circle the block a few times because his medication hadn't yet started working and he was shaking quite a bit. A similar thing happened to him later that year when he was backstage at the *Late Show with David Letterman* show waiting for his medication to kick in, hoping it would work in time for him to make his appearance.

The constant worry and fear that he would be seen showing symptoms of Parkinson's, or that a tabloid magazine would reveal his secret, wore on Fox. There had been rumors in gossip columns in 1997 that something might be wrong with him, probably because he had been spotted in a doctor's office. In 1998, a few tabloid magazines began hounding him about the rumors, including a reporter

At the 1998 Golden Globe Awards in Los Angeles, Fox shows off his award for his role on the television sitcom *Spin City*.

who accosted him outside his apartment one morning when he was taking Sam to school. Although the tabloids didn't print the story because they had no proof of what was wrong with him, Fox knew that it might not be long before they did find out he had Parkinson's disease. And he wanted to make the announcement on his own terms, not on the terms of a tabloid.

Fox began to think life would be much easier for him and for his family and the few other people who did know his secret if he made his Parkinson's diagnosis public. Still, he worried that people would have a hard time laughing at his character on *Spin City* (or in any movies or television shows he might do in the future) if they were too busy feeling sorry for him or too distracted by looking for signs of his Parkinson's disease. He was also concerned about how revealing his secret might affect his children. Would their schoolmates, friends, and teachers tease them or misunderstand Parkinson's disease?

After months of weighing whether to reveal his diagnosis, Fox finally came to the decision to make his Parkinson's disease public knowledge. Keeping his secret seemed more trouble than it was worth. "I was

**Janet Reno**

Janet Reno is a lawyer, the first woman to become attorney general of the United States, and a Parkinson's patient. In 1995, Reno was diagnosed with Parkinson's at age fifty-seven, while serving as attorney general. Reno chose to announce her diagnosis right away and did not try to hide her symptoms. She continued to do her job and make appearances at conferences and fund-raisers, serving as attorney general until 2001.

simply tired of hiding the truth from people and felt ready, finally, to present it to them on my own terms, with the hope that they'd respond to my story in the spirit in which it was offered," Fox wrote in *Lucky Man*.

## Going Public

Fox chose to tell his story to *People* magazine and to Barbara Walters on the television newsmagazine *20/20*. His revelation appeared on the *People* magazine Web site the day before Thanksgiving in November 1998. In his *People* interview, Fox emphasized his positive outlook, saying, "The biggest thing is that I can be in this situation and still love life as much as I do. Life is great."

Almost immediately after the story hit the *People* Web site, the news was posted on other Web sites and then on television stations' nightly newscasts and in newspapers the following day. Fox's phone began ringing off the hook. His publicist received hundreds of requests from people wanting to interview Fox.

Fox had expected a certain amount of reaction to his story, especially from entertainment magazines and television shows. However, the revelation about his diagnosis became a news story as well, and the attention it focused on Parkinson's disease was enormous. Many newspapers, magazines, and television shows ran additional stories with information about the disease.

The Monday following Thanksgiving, Fox taped his interview with Barbara Walters for *20/20*. The Thanksgiving weekend had been filled with stories about him and he found the intense attention a bit overwhelming. Before the interview began, Walters reassured Fox that the reason for all the attention was that the public had "known" the actor—at least a version of him they thought they knew from seeing him on television and movie screens—for so many years. They cared about him. She also emphasized that his revelation was a chance for people to learn more about the disease.

When the interview with Walters appeared on television that Friday night, 16.5 million people tuned in to see Fox talk about his diagnosis and the way he had kept it secret. He was very upbeat during the interview, and near the end, he emphasized that he was sure that researchers would find a cure for Parkinson's soon and he and other Parkinson's patients would someday be cured.

## Shining a Light

While Fox was flattered by the attention his story received and the care and concern people he didn't even know were showing for him, he was far more gratified by something else: his story was shining a light on Parkinson's disease and the millions of people around the world who have Parkinson's. Fox began to hear how much telling his story had helped other Parkinson's patients. The publicity had made the disease much more well known and better understood.

Several years after Fox revealed his Parkinson's diagnosis to Barbara Walters, he talked to Walters again, this time about his book *Lucky Man*.

Many other people had kept their Parkinson's diagnosis secret because they were afraid of losing their jobs or being seen as a freak, but once Fox told his story, it was easier for people to share their stories with friends or coworkers. Fox got many calls and e-mails from people thanking him for going public.

People who worked for Parkinson's organizations or groups that assist people with disabilities recognized Fox's bravery in going public. Jim Dickson, the vice president of the National Organization on Disability told *WE* magazine in January 1999, "It takes courage to come out and say you've got any disability, particularly when you still have the option to hide it, and [Fox] should be applauded for putting it on the line, especially in the entertainment world."

Parkinson's activists were thankful for the attention now focused on the disease, and many realized that Fox was the perfect spokesperson for the Parkinson's cause. Dr. Abraham Lieberman of the National Parkinson Foundation told *WE* magazine in January 1999 that Fox drew attention to Parkinson's like "a magnet because he's perceived as a good person, everyone's younger brother."

As much as telling his story helped other people, it also helped Fox himself. Because he had kept quiet about his diagnosis, in a way he had felt very alone. Once other people began sharing their stories with him, he knew he was not the only person struggling with Parkinson's. He had grown up a lot in the seven years since he had been diagnosed with Parkinson's, but he grew even more after going public. He wrote in *Lucky Man*, "I'm grateful I didn't wait any longer to share my story. To do so would have been to deprive myself of what has been one of the most rewarding—and educational—experiences of my life."

## Two Turning Points

On September 28, 1999, a little less than a year after he made his diagnosis public, Fox testified at a hearing in the U.S. Senate about government funding for Parkinson's disease research. Fox, along with other Parkinson's patients, activists, and researchers, urged the Senate to set aside more money for research into a cure for Parkinson's. Many scientists working to find a cure felt that it was within reach if more money was put toward the effort. At the hearing, Fox declared, "The war against Parkinson's is a winnable war, and I have resolved to play a role in that victory."

With that declaration, Fox started on a new path. After his revelation about his diagnosis, he had thought about getting involved in the fight to cure Parkinson's. After his Senate testimony, he told *Town & Country* magazine in June 2006 that he thought, "Don't I have a responsibility to do something about this, whether I want to or not?"

At his first Senate appearance, in September 1999, Fox said, "The one million Americans living with Parkinson's want to beat this disease, but it won't happen until Congress adequately funds Parkinson's research."

At first, he wasn't sure exactly how to proceed. But with the amazing amount of interest now focused on Parkinson's due to the interest in him as a celebrity, he knew he had to do something.

His Senate appearance drove this point home because $10 million in additional funding went to Parkinson's research partly as a result of his testimony. Unfortunately, this was only a fraction of what Fox had requested ($75 million), and researchers said at the time that as much as $244 million was needed.

Parkinson's groups large and small got in touch with him in the year after he announced his diagnosis. He was surprised by how many different Parkinson's organizations there were, and he was disappointed that none of the organizations seemed to be working together to find a cure. In fact, the organizations were competitive; one even told him if he wouldn't help their organization, he shouldn't help a rival organization either.

Fox continued to mull over how he should get involved, but he was kept busy with his work on *Spin City*. Before Fox went public with his diagnosis, he had made some changes in his work life. Although the surgery he had had in March 1998 helped stop the tremors on the left-hand side of his body, by the spring of 1999—after another long year of working on *Spin City*—he was feeling more tired than usual and his symptoms had gotten worse. By then, Fox was the producer of the show, so he had even more duties in addition to his starring role. He decided to add a new star to the cast of *Spin City* and lessen his role a bit. He chose actress Heather Locklear, and she began work in the fall of 1999. However, that season of *Spin City* was still tiring for the actor.

While on vacation with his family in January 2000, Fox noticed that his Parkinson's symptoms were less severe. He realized that acting in and pro-ducing a television show were very stressful, so he came to a decision: he would retire from *Spin City* at the end of that season.

Retiring from *Spin City* would not only allow him to relax more and spend more time with his family, but it would also give him time to become more involved in the Parkinson's cause. He felt that he wouldn't be able to do both things—act and be an activist—equally well, and it was time to focus on the

After four seasons of starring in *Spin City*, Fox retired from acting and producing the show in May 2000. He made some guest appearances on the sitcom the following year.

higher priority. As he told *Newsweek* magazine in May 2000, "It's not that I couldn't have continued [with *Spin City*]. It just seemed kind of pointless, given that I have an opportunity to help."

On January 18, 2000, Fox announced his retirement from *Spin City*. That same day, he called Joan Samuelson of the Parkinson's Action Network to tell her he was ready to do more for the cause. The

DATE _11/22/99_

rk $ 25,000.00

nd DOLLARS

Fox worked with Joan Samuelson *(right)* of the Parkinson's Action Network to bring greater awareness to the cause.

Parkinson's Action Network brings awareness to the disease, helps patients, and raises government money for research. Fox had met Samuelson when he testified in the Senate in September 1999.

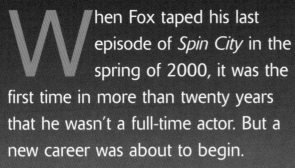

# CHAPTER FOUR

## From Actor to Activist

When Fox taped his last episode of *Spin City* in the spring of 2000, it was the first time in more than twenty years that he wasn't a full-time actor. But a new career was about to begin.

As Fox had determined the year before, he wanted to become more involved in the fight to cure Parkinson's disease. However, he remained unsure about how best to do that. He continued to do some work for the Parkinson's Action Network, and he began learning as much as possible about the disease and about research that might lead to new treatments or to a cure by talking to scientists and experts in the field.

Fox also testified again in the U.S. Senate on September 14, 2000, to lobby for more funding for Parkinson's research. He told the senators stories of others who had Parkinson's and described how having Parkinson's affected their lives.

After telling the stories of others with Parkinson's, Fox discussed the fact that his celebrity as an actor brought him more attention than the everyday people he had just described. But, he testified, "None of

Stress can make Parkinson's symptoms worse, so giving a speech can be a challenge for Fox and others with the disease.

these people mind that I get more attention than they do. What they tell me, over and over, is that if I get a shot in front of a microphone—I should start talking. So here I am."

## Putting His Fame to Good Use

When Fox thought about how to use the fact that he was a celebrity to help the cause of Parkinson's research, he decided he didn't want to be just a face on a poster that an existing Parkinson's fund-raising group could use to draw attention to the cause. He wanted to be able to have input in making decisions about how the money raised would be used.

Although Fox was initially hesitant to use his celebrity status to his advantage, he had begun to realize that there was no better way to use his fame. He discussed this in his autobiography, *Lucky Man*:

> *My name attracts attention, provides access, and helps [us meet goals] faster. Is this fair? Is this right? Well, that's complicated . . . but the fact remains:* **I have this disease.** *This is not a* role *I'm playing . . . I know the issues, I'm [learning] the science, and I share my*

*community's sense of urgency. I [also] happen to possess this most rare and useful currency—celebrity—and I've discovered a wonderful way to spend it.*

At first, Fox had no plans to start his own Parkinson's organization, but as he considered the issue, he began to realize that it would be the best way to have a say in how things would be run and how money would be distributed. In a March 2005 interview with *Chronicle of Philanthropy* magazine, Fox reflected on how he came to the decision to start his own organization: "I thought, if I'm going to be talking to people and asking them to make a commitment—financial, emotional, intellectual, or otherwise—I better be able to put the full weight of everything I stand for behind that commitment and behind that relationship."

With the decision to start his own Parkinson's foundation behind him, he had many decisions in front of him. What would the group be called? Who would run the foundation? How would the group raise money? How would it distribute the money it raised?

**Michael J. Fox, Author**

In 2002, Fox published *Lucky Man*, his first book. Because it is difficult for him to type, he dictated the book to an assistant. She typed as he spoke and would later print out their day's work. He would then edit what he had "written." Fox is now working on a second book called *Always Looking Up*. It is about his positive outlook on life, and the title is a joke about the fact that he is not so tall (about five feet, four inches).

## Building the Foundation

There was a lot to think about, and one of the first decisions to make was what to call the foundation. One of Fox's first ideas was PDCure (for Parkinson's Disease Cure), but his wife pointed out that it sounded a lot like "pedicure." Eventually, Fox settled on the Michael J. Fox Foundation for Parkinson's Research. He hadn't intended to name the foundation after himself, but he realized that his name would call attention to the cause, which was one of his goals. In May 2000, Fox announced that he was

The Web site for the Michael J. Fox Foundation (http://www.michaeljfox.org) has a wealth of information for Parkinson's patients, researchers, and anyone interested in getting involved in the cause.

starting the Michael J. Fox Foundation for Parkinson's Research.

In addition to drawing attention to Parkinson's disease, Fox's main goal for the foundation was to find a cure for Parkinson's within ten years. Many scientists had told him that a cure was close, and Fox was optimistic that a cure could be found. He hoped that the Michael J. Fox Foundation would be out of business by 2010 because its work to find a cure would by then be completed.

Although scientists felt confident that a cure for Parkinson's could be found within ten years, what they lacked was the money needed to make that happen. Scientists were getting some funding from the U.S. government through the National Institutes of Health, but they were not getting nearly enough.

Another problem Fox saw with government funding was that it took up to a year from the time a scientist submitted a research idea to the government to the time he or she got the money to begin doing research (if the government approved the research idea in the first place). Applying for the funding could also be a complicated and long process. Fox wanted to fix those problems by giving away as much money as possible, as quickly and easily as possible.

With the foundation established and the goals decided, Fox began the search for people to help him run the Michael J. Fox Foundation. Fox realized that he didn't have the experience to run the foundation on his own—and didn't want to even if he could. He had quit *Spin City* to be able to spend more time enjoying himself with his family, and he didn't want to trade one full-time job for another. Fox also realized that he wasn't the right person to run the organization day to day. In a June 2006 interview with *Town & Country* magazine, he described his decision to hire someone to run the foundation: "I have no management skills, but I realized I only had to be smart enough to find people who are smarter than me and keep them close."

Fox got some help finding someone smarter than he was from an unlikely source. At the time when Fox had first announced that he had Parkinson's, his twin daughters were in nursery school. Some of the parents of other children who attended the nursery school asked him then if there was anything they could do to help him. At the time, he thanked them for their offers but said there was nothing they could do. However, Fox remembered their offers of help when he was setting up the Michael J. Fox Foundation. Many of the parents had jobs in finance and offered to get involved in the foundation. Others suggested people who might be able to run the foundation. One of them suggested Deborah Brooks, who had worked as an investment banker for many years but had quit to work with two nonprofit organizations.

When Fox interviewed Brooks to be the chief executive officer (CEO) of the Michael J. Fox Foundation, he immediately knew she would be perfect. He quickly hired her and joked that he would have to fire her if she still had the job in ten years because by then they both hoped that there would be a cure for Parkinson's. Brooks began work in October 2000.

## Funding the Foundation

With Brooks on board to help him set up and eventually run the Michael J. Fox Foundation, Fox began working out the practical details of how the foundation would work. One thing they needed to figure out was how they would raise money to fund the research they wanted to support.

With his successes in television and movies, Fox was financially well off and could afford to contribute money to fund Parkinson's research. However, one of the points of starting a foundation was to raise as much money as possible; therefore, Fox would need to get financial contributions from others to make

Jimmy Kimmel is just one of many celebrities who have donated time and money to Fox's foundation at the annual A Funny Thing Happened on the Way to Cure Parkinson's. Kimmel hosted the event in 2005.

the Michael J. Fox Foundation a success. (Although Fox has contributed his own money to the foundation, he doesn't specify how much. He says that he contributes money from time to time to fund special projects. Also, he gave all of the money he made from the sales of his autobiography, *Lucky Man—* more than $3 million—to the foundation.)

One way to consistently raise money is to have annual fund-raising events, and the Michael J. Fox Foundation decided to have several each year. One of its major events is called A Funny Thing Happened on the Way to Cure Parkinson's. Beginning in 2000, it has been held every year in New York City. Actors, athletes, comedians, and rock stars attend and perform at the event, and so far, this event alone has raised more than $20 million for the Michael J. Fox Foundation. In 2005, the foundation added a similar annual event called A Sunny Thing Happened on the Way to Cure Parkinson's. This event is held in Los Angeles each spring, and in its first year, the event raised $6.4 million.

The Michael J. Fox Foundation also hosts a golf event fund-raiser each year in September, participates in the Parkinson's Unity Walk in New York City each

The November 2006 A Funny Thing Happened on the Way to Cure Parkinson's raised almost $5.7 million in just one night.

spring, and sometimes auctions celebrity items to raise additional money. It also holds joint fund-raisers, such as Betting on a Cause and a Cure, a casino night cosponsored by the Cam Neely Foundation for Cancer Care and the Leary Firefighters Foundation.

Although the Michael J. Fox Foundation gets large contributions from very wealthy people, it also gets many contributions in smaller amounts from "regular" people who aren't extremely wealthy. A foundation program called Team Fox helps individuals organize local fund-raisers such as bike races, marathons, golf events, and bake sales. Team Fox began in 2006 and raised $1 million in its first year.

## Spending the Money

Since neither Fox nor Deborah Brooks had ever run a charity organization, they needed some help in establishing procedures so that the Michael J. Fox Foundation could be a success. They turned to many people for help. To advise them and help run the foundation, they recruited financial professionals, philanthropists, and people who knew (or were themselves) Parkinson's patients to join the board of directors.

To give them insight into how to set up and run a charitable foundation, Fox and Brooks met with Christopher Reeve, the actor known for playing Superman who had set up the Christopher Reeve Paralysis Foundation after becoming paralyzed in a horseback-riding accident in 1995. They also met with Michael Milken, a well-known financial executive who had started the Prostate Cancer Foundation after developing prostate cancer in 1993. For his

One of Fox's role models in celebrity activism was Christopher Reeve, pictured here with his wife, Dana, in 2003. Although Reeve died in 2004, his foundation continues to raise money to fund research into curing paralysis.

Prostate Cancer Foundation, Milken had created a process to get money to cancer researchers quickly, and Fox and Brooks wanted to do something similar with the Michael J. Fox Foundation as part of their goal to get money to Parkinson's disease researchers as quickly as possible.

With help from Milken and several other experienced professionals, the Michael J. Fox Foundation developed a process to cut down the amount of time it would take for scientists to receive money for Parkinson's research. The normal process took as much as one year, and the Michael J. Fox Foundation was able to reduce the time to just three months. To do this, it shortened the application forms scientists had to fill out, made the rest of the process of applying for funding easier, and put together a committee to review and quickly decide on the scientists' proposals.

J. William Langston joined the Michael J. Fox Foundation as the scientific adviser, and he heads the review committee, which is made up of a team of leading scientists and other professionals from all over the world. The group meets fifteen to twenty times each year to make funding decisions. The

Tennis star Andre Agassi *(left)* took part in a conference in California in April 2007 with Fox and Michael Milken *(right)* to discuss the role of public figures in raising money for research, education, and other social causes.

committee also discusses potential Parkinson's research, looking for important areas in which research does not seem to be moving quickly enough. It targets those areas by putting money aside for research working on that topic, and it also tries to find ways to get research moving in that direction. In addition, the committee reviews and discusses recent discoveries in Parkinson's research. It has also developed a program called Linked Efforts to Accelerate Parkinson's Solutions (LEAPS). This program gives money to scientists who are working together on joint Parkinson's research projects.

By April 2001, less than a year after its founding, the Michael J. Fox Foundation granted $1.5 million to Parkinson's researchers in Canada, Germany, Spain, and the United States. Fox was extremely gratified that the foundation was able to make a difference so soon after it started, and in a press release the foundation issued on April 1, Fox called the grants "an exciting first-step in our Foundation's active involvement in the search for a Parkinson's cure."

Many scientists had applied to the foundation for funding, and Fox considered that evidence that Parkinson's could be cured if funding reached the right people. In the press release, Fox also confirmed that "the Foundation remains committed to supporting as much research as possible—and to that end we hope to make additional awards within the next few months."

# CHAPTER FIVE

## The Future of Parkinson's

The Michael J. Fox Foundation's biggest annual fund-raising event, A Funny Thing Happened on the Way to Cure Parkinson's, is just one example of the amazing success the foundation has achieved in the years since Fox started the organization. Each November, the event raises several million dollars for Parkinson's—in 2006, it raised almost $6 million. Other fund-raising events are equally successful, and the foundation also receives money from individuals— and even children—through local fund-raising events.

Of the money raised through all aspects of the Michael J. Fox Foundation, almost 85 cents of every dollar goes directly to scientists doing Parkinson's research. Since the foundation began in 2000, it has given nearly $90 million to Parkinson's researchers. Other than the U.S. government, the foundation has given more than any other organization to Parkinson's research.

## The Foundation Today

The Michael J. Fox Foundation has grown into a successful and extremely well-respected organization. It has funded many important research projects. Scientists who have gotten funding from the foundation are grateful not only for the money they have received but also for the way the foundation operates. By getting them money quickly and efficiently, scientists are able to spend less time on paperwork and more time on research. The foundation has also helped scientists team up with other researchers who may be working on similar projects, allowing them to use their combined brainpower to solve problems and make scientific breakthroughs.

Deborah Brooks ran the foundation as CEO until February 2007. In March, a new CEO—Sarah Orsay—took over. Fox talks with the foundation CEO a few

**How You Can Get Involved**

A branch of Team Fox called Students Give Back (SGB) is a program that allows students from elementary school up through college to hold local fund-raisers. SGB gives students tools and advice for planning and hosting various events to raise money for the foundation, such as a popular pancake breakfast fund-raiser called Pancakes for Parkinson's. To learn more about Students Give Back, check the Team Fox Web site (http://www.teamfox.org).

times a week and keeps track of current research but leaves the management of the foundation to Orsay. As he told *Chronicle of Philanthropy* magazine in March 2005, "The best thing I can do is be willing to get out of the way. But when I'm supposed to get in the way, I want to provide a meaningful presence."

Fox goes to meetings at the foundation offices, but he also has his own office in the building where he lives, near Central Park in New York City. Fox attends fund-raising events, continues to lobby the U.S. government for increased funding for Parkinson's research, and pushes for funding in other ways. For example, he wrote an article for *Forbes* (a financial magazine) in May 2007 encouraging people to use money wisely for research into Parkinson's and other diseases.

Tracy Pollan, Fox's wife, serves on the board of directors of the foundation, and even his children are involved. Fox's oldest child, Sam, volunteers by helping with the foundation's computer database.

## Stem Cell Controversy

In 2006, Fox found himself in the middle of the stem cell debate. Stem cells are cells that have the potential to produce other, specialized cells such as heart cells or brain cells. Scientists have long believed that stem cells could potentially cure diseases such as Alzheimer's, multiple sclerosis, Parkinson's, and many others.

There are three types of stem cells: embryonic, which come from blastocysts (recently fertilized human eggs); adult, which come from bone marrow and a few other types of tissue; and cord blood, which come from the umbilical cord. Embryonic stem cells are the easiest to turn into other specific types of cells to potentially repair damaged tissue in

In addition to her work at the Fox Foundation and raising four children, Tracy Pollan has continued to act and was nominated for an Emmy for her appearance on *Law & Order: Special Victims Unit* in 1999.

the brain and many other places. For example, embryonic stem cells could be turned into spinal cord tissue to help people who are paralyzed regain the ability to move. Embryonic stem cells could also potentially be turned into the dopamine-producing cells in the brain that are damaged in Parkinson's patients.

However, some people are opposed to the use of embryonic stem cells because these embryos are fertilized eggs and therefore have the potential to become a human being. Scientists would like to use embryos that have been produced at fertility clinics and are not being used, but the law prevents this. At the present time, scientists can use cells from only twenty-two sources that were set aside by President George W. Bush in 2001.

Because embryonic stem cells could potentially treat or cure Parkinson's, Fox has long tried to get the U.S. government to change its policy on the use of embryonic stem cells. During the 2006 congressional campaign, Fox helped congressional candidates who favored increased use of stem cell research. He appeared at campaign rallies, made campaign ads, and did television interviews in support

Since writing a *New York Times* editorial before the 2000 presidential election, Fox has actively supported stem cell research. Here, he campaigns with Senator Jim Webb in November 2006.

of the candidates. Many people praised his efforts to call attention to the stem cell debate, but pro-life activists criticized him for his participation in the congressional campaign, saying that using stem cells destroys human life.

One of the harshest critics of Fox's 2006 campaign activism was Rush Limbaugh, a conservative Republican talk-show host. Limbaugh accused Fox of not taking his medication, or faking his Parkinson's symptoms during campaign appearances and in television ads, in which you could see his arms and upper body moving uncontrollably. People close to Fox, particularly his mother, were outraged at Limbaugh's personal attacks and suggestions that Fox was faking his symptoms. Fox, however, took the attacks in stride and tried to ignore the criticism and focus instead on the increased attention the attacks brought to the stem cell debate.

While Fox continues to back any politician—Democrat or Republican—who supports the increased use of stem cells, the Michael J. Fox Foundation is funding ongoing stem cell

At a July 2005 news conference to promote a Senate act that would have provided additional funding for stem cell research, Fox conferred with Senator Orrin Hatch.

research that makes use of the approved twenty-two stem cell sources. However, research on stem cells is just one of the many types of research the foundation supports.

## Happy to Be of Service

Although Fox no longer considers himself part of the entertainment industry, since retiring from *Spin City* he has kept busy with some acting and voice-over work. He was the voice of Stuart in the three *Stuart Little* movies and had voice-over roles in *Homeward Bound* and *Atlantis: The Lost Empire*. Fox has also appeared on television as a guest star for two episodes of *Scrubs* in 2004 and six episodes of *Boston Legal* in 2006.

Fox has won many awards for his television and movie acting, including four Emmy Awards, four Golden Globes, two Screen Actors Guild Awards, and several awards from other organizations. He got a star on the Hollywood Walk of Fame on December 16, 2002. He also became an American citizen in 2000.

Although his Parkinson's symptoms sometimes get in the way, Fox skis, ice-skates, plays tennis, and

### Awakenings

In the late 1910s, millions of people around the world got a virus called encephalitis, or sleeping sickness. About 30 percent died, and of those who recovered, many fell into a coma-like state with symptoms similar to those of Parkinson's. Some remained in a coma for years, and in 1969, Dr. Oliver Sacks gave some of these patients levodopa, the drug used to treat Parkinson's. The patients awoke and seemed free of symptoms. While their "awakening" didn't last, the fact that levodopa worked could suggest that a similar virus causes Parkinson's. Dr. Sacks's experiment with these patients is the subject of his 1973 book *Awakenings* and a 1990 movie starring Robin Williams and Robert DeNiro.

goes scuba diving. In the summer, Fox and his family vacation on Martha's Vineyard. Winter vacations are spent in Vermont or Connecticut.

Fox is a celebrity and an activist, but in many ways, he leads a regular life. He and his family go out to dinner or to the movies. He helps his four children (Fox and Pollan had a fourth child, daughter Esmé, in 2001) with their homework and their after-school

Combining his love of hockey with his willingness to help charitable causes, Fox has skated in several celebrity hockey tournaments, including Denis Leary's Celebrity Hat Trick, which raises money for fire departments.

activities like sports and music. His kids don't make a big deal about the fact that he is a celebrity or that he has Parkinson's. He is just their dad—the same dad they've always known. Fox remains very much in love with Tracy Pollan and credits her with being a great partner in everything he does. She always gives him wonderful advice and helps keep him grounded. Aside from his family, the thing that makes him happiest is his work with the Michael J. Fox Foundation. "To be able to be of service, to help people, that's the greatest privilege I could have," he told *People* magazine in November 2006.

When he created the Michael J. Fox Foundation for Parkinson's Research in 2000, Fox knew that it would attract attention because he was a well-known actor. However, he was determined to make it a serious organization and not just a celebrity cause that he could work on for a few hours a year. Because he had a goal—to cure Parkinson's disease— that was extremely important and very personal to him, he was willing to make the effort to turn the foundation into a successful organization.

Through his hard work, the foundation has not only funded millions of dollars worth of research

projects, but it has also made Parkinson's a household word and has gotten thousands of people involved in the cause. Oliver Sacks, a noted neurologist, writer, and researcher, explained to *People* magazine in November 2006 that Fox "has done more than any other person on this planet to [call attention to Parkinson's disease]."

Because Parkinson's disease is progressive, Fox's symptoms have gotten worse over time, and the medication he takes to treat the disease has become less effective. However, Fox spends very little time worrying about what might happen as his symptoms continue to progress.

Fox tries to enjoy as normal a life as possible. Here, he, his wife, and two of their daughters watch a tennis match at the 2006 U.S. Open.

Fox is pleased that something positive has come of his Parkinson's diagnosis. One of his proudest achievements is that the Fox Foundation is a well-respected organization that does not rely on his name for its solid reputation.

He doesn't see any point in that; instead, he looks ahead to the future with hope for a cure for Parkinson's. One of his goals in founding the Michael J. Fox Foundation in 2000 was to find a cure within ten years. In March 2005, he talked to *Chronicles of Philanthropy* magazine about the chances of that happening: "If we haven't cured it by 2010, we'll be on the way. And if it takes us 15 years, are we going to consider ourselves failures? No. We're going to feel pretty good."

Even if a cure for Parkinson's is not found in time to meet his 2010 goal, it's likely that Fox will remain as positive and upbeat as he has always been. He has led a happy and fulfilling life with his family and has found great success with his television and movie roles, and his foundation has made great strides toward changing the lives of millions of people with Parkinson's disease.

Although Parkinson's has changed Fox's life, he chooses to look at it as changing his life in a good way. "I've gotten a lot, for one human being," he told *Town & Country* magazine in June 2006. "The shaking and not always being able to do what I want to do—it's not that bad. I don't feel anger; I don't feel fear. I have a full life. I don't look at the world through PD-colored glasses. I look at the world the way I've always looked at the world: I feel really lucky."

# GLOSSARY

**accost**  To approach and speak to someone in a challenging way.

**Alzheimer's disease**  A brain disease that causes loss of memory and mental abilities.

**audition**  To try out to get a part in a play, television show, movie, or other performance.

**chief executive officer (CEO)**  The person responsible for overseeing a business.

**database**  A collection of information stored on a computer that can be sorted and arranged.

**dyskinesia**  Difficulty controlling movements; a tic.

**encrypt**  To code information so it cannot be used by others.

**lobby**  To try to influence lawmakers or public officials.

**multiple sclerosis**  A brain disease that causes partial paralysis.

**neurologist**  A doctor who specializes in diagnosing and treating brain and nervous system disorders.

**neurotransmitter**  A substance in the brain that carries an impulse from one nerve to another.

**pacemaker**  An electrical device that steadies the heart's rhythm.

**philanthropist**  Someone who raises money for or gives donations to charitable causes.

**physical therapy**  Treatment by massage, exercise, heat, or water.

**probe**  A medical instrument that can be inserted into the brain.

**propensity**  A natural inclination toward or liking for something.

**stature**  Height of a person.

**tremor**  Trembling or shaking, usually caused by a disease.

# FOR MORE INFORMATION

American Parkinson Disease Association
135 Parkinson Avenue
Staten Island, NY 10305-1425
(800) 223-2732
Web site: http://www.apdaparkinson.org
The American Parkinson Disease Association (APDA)
is the country's largest grassroots organization
serving the 1.5 million Americans with Parkinson's
disease and their caregivers in three vital areas:
research, patient and caregiver support, and
education.

Michael J. Fox Foundation for Parkinson's Research
Grand Central Station
P.O. Box 4777
New York, NY 10163
(212) 509-0995
Web site: http://www.michaeljfox.org
The Michael J. Fox Foundation raises funds that go
directly to fund research into causes and cures
for Parkinson's disease.

National Parkinson Foundation
1501 NW 9th Avenue
Bob Hope Road
Miami, FL 33136-1494
(800) 327-4545
Web site: http://www.parkinson.org
The National Parkinson Foundation (NPF) is the
largest and oldest national Parkinson foundation
in the United States. NPF supports Parkinson-
related research, patient care, education, training,
and outreach.

Parkinson Alliance
P.O. Box 308
Kingston, NJ 08528-0308
(800) 579-8440
Web site: http://www.parkinsonalliance.org
Parkinson Alliance is a national nonprofit organization dedicated to raising funds to help finance
the most promising research to find the cause
and cure for Parkinson's disease. The Alliance
runs the annual Parkinson's Unity Walk in New
York City.

Parkinson's Action Network
1025 Vermont Avenue NW
Suite 1120
Washington, DC 20005
(800) 850-4726
Web site: http://www.parkinsonsaction.org
Parkinson's Action Network (PAN) is an advocacy
   group that lobbies in Washington, D.C., for
   Parkinson's-related causes.

Parkinson's Disease Foundation
1359 Broadway, Suite 1509
New York, NY 10018
(800) 457-6676
Web site: http://www.pdf.org
The Parkinson's Disease Foundation (PDF) is a leading
   national presence in Parkinson's disease research,
   education, and public advocacy.

Parkinson's Institute
1170 Morse Avenue
Sunnyvale, CA 94089-1605
(800) 786-2958

Web site: http://www.thepi.org

The Parkinson's Institute has a movement disorders patient clinic, a research laboratory, and specialized services, education, and outreach programs.

Parkinson Society Canada
4211 Yonge Street, Suite 316
Toronto, ON M2P 2A9
Canada
(800) 565-3000
Web site: http://www.parkinson.ca

Parkinson Society Canada (PSC) is a national, not-for-profit, volunteer-based charity with more than one hundred chapters and many support groups working nationwide.

Victoria Epilepsy & Parkinson's Centre (VEPC)
813 Darwin Avenue
Victoria, BC, Canada  V8X 2X7
(250) 475-6677
Web site: http://www.vepc.bc.ca

The VEPC is dedicated to enhancing quality of life for those whose lives are touched by epilepsy or Parkinson's.

# Web Sites

Due to the changing nature of Internet links, Rosen Publishing has developed an online list of Web sites related to the subject of this book. This site is updated regularly. Please use this link to access the list:

http://www.rosenlinks.com/cea/mifo

# FOR FURTHER READING

Abramovitz, Melissa. *Parkinson's Disease*. San Diego, CA: Lucent Books, 2005.

Black, Laura. *The Stem Cell Debate: The Ethics and Science Behind the Research*. Berkeley Heights, NJ: Enslow Publishers, 2006.

Kozar, Richard. *Michael J. Fox: Overcoming Adversity*. Philadelphia, PA: Chelsea House Publishers, 1999.

Kramer, Barbara. *Michael J. Fox: Courage for Life*. Berkeley Heights, NJ: Enslow Publishers, 2005.

Mosley, Anthony D., and Deborah S. Romaine. *The A to Z of Parkinson's Disease*. New York, NY: Facts On File, 2004.

Panno, Joseph. *Stem Cell Research: Medical Applications and Ethical Controversy*. New York, NY: Facts On File, 2005.

Silverstein, Alvin, Virginia Silverstein, and Laura Silverstein Nunn. *Parkinson's Disease*. Berkeley Heights, NJ: Enslow Publishers, 2002.

Vander Hook, Sue. *Parkinson's Disease*. North Mankato, MN: Smart Apple Media, 2001.

Wheeler, Jill. *Michael J. Fox*. Edina, MN: ABDO Publishing Company, 2001.

# BIBLIOGRAPHY

Abramovitz, Melissa. *Parkinson's Disease*. San Diego, CA: Lucent Books, 2005.

Bennetts, Leslie. "Character Study." *Town & Country*, June 2006.

Brennen, Jensen. "Acting with Intent." *Chronicle of Philanthropy*, March 31, 2005.

Cowley, Geoffrey, Andrew Murr, Marc Peyser, and Rat Sawhill. "The New War on Parkinson's." *Newsweek*, May 22, 2000.

Fox, Michael J. *Lucky Man: A Memoir*. New York, NY: Hyperion, 2002.

Hammonds, Keith H. "Change Agents—Michael J. Fox and Deborah Brooks." *Fast Company*, October 2001.

Johnson, Brian D. "Michael Then and Now." *Maclean's*, April 29, 2002.

Kozar, Richard. *Michael J. Fox: Overcoming Adversity*. Philadelphia, PA: Chelsea House Publishers, 1999.

*Maclean's*. "The Mysterious Vancouver Connection." April 29, 2002.

Peyser, Mark. "It's Like Everything—You Just Roll with It." *Newsweek*, May 22, 2000.

Riley, Charles A. "Into the Maelstrom." *WE Magazine*, January/February 1999.

Schindehette, Susan, Mike Lipton, Lauren Comander, Mary Green, and Kathy Ehrich Dowd. "I'm So Blessed." *People*, November 13, 2006.

Schneider, Karen S., and Todd Gold. "After the Tears." *People*, December 7, 1998.

Schneider, Karen S., Cynthia Wang, Fannie Weinstein, Elizabeth McNeil, Ken Baker, Tom Cunneff, Ulrica Wihlborg, Jane Sims Podesta, and Karen Ann Cullotta. "Real-Life Family Ties." *People*, February 7, 2000.

Seccombe, Mike. "Michael J. Fox Paces Through Life of Writing." *Vineyard Gazette*, August 3, 2007.

Silverstein, Alvin, Virginia Silverstein, and Laura Silverstein Nunn. *Parkinson's Disease*. Berkeley Heights, NJ: Enslow Publishers, 2002.

Vander Hook, Sue. *Parkinson's Disease*. North Mankato, MN: Smart Apple Media, 2001.

# INDEX

## About the Author

Simone Payment has a degree in psychology from Cornell University and a master's degree in elementary education from Wheelock College. She is the author of eighteen books for young adults. Her book *Inside Special Operations: Navy SEALs* (also from Rosen Publishing) won a 2004 Quick Picks for Reluctant Young Readers Award from the American Library Association and is on the Nonfiction Honor List of Voice of Youth Advocates. She hopes the Michael J. Fox Foundation is successful in its attempt to cure Parkinson's because her father is one of the many Americans who has the disease.

## Photo Credits

Designer: Tahara Anderson; Editor: Nicholas Croce